53 Interesting Ways to Promote Equal Opportunities in Education

Vicky Lewis

and

Sue Habeshaw

First published in 1990 by
Technical and Educational Services Ltd.
37 Ravenswood Road
Bristol BS6 6BW
UK

Revised edition 1995

ISBN 0 947885 51 X

Printed in Great Britain by The Cromwell Press Ltd., Melksham, Wilts.

Other books by Technical and Educational Services

53 Interesting Things to Do in Your Lectures
53 Interesting Things to Do in Your Seminars and Tutorials
53 Interesting Ways to Assess Your Students
53 Interesting Ways of Helping Your Students to Study
53 Interesting Communication Exercises for Science Students
53 Interesting Ways to Appraise Your Teaching
53 Interesting Ways to Teach Mathematics
53 Interesting Problems with Large Classes: Making the Best of a Bad Job
53 Interesting Ways to Write Open Learning Materials
53 Interesting Activities for Open Learning Courses
Preparing to Teach: An Introduction to Effective Teaching in Higher Education
253 Ideas for Your Teaching
Interesting Ways to Teach: 12 Do-It-Yourself Staff Development Exercises
Creating a Teaching Profile
Getting the Most from Your Data: Practical Ideas on how to Analyse Qualitative Data
Writing Study Guides
Improving the Quality of Student Learning
HMA Stationery Ltd

The authors

Photograph by Andrew Squires

Vicky Lewis is a Lecturer in the Department of Psychology at Warwick University. She is a developmental psychologist with particular interest in children with special educational needs and is the author of *Development and Handicap* (Blackwell, 1987). She runs workshops on study skills, supervising research students and equal opportunities.

Sue Habeshaw is a Senior Lecturer and Course Advisor in the Faculty of Humanities at the University of the West of England. She teaches literature, drama, study skills and various aspects of personal development including co-counselling and assertiveness. She is co-author of nine books in the series *Interesting Ways to Teach*.

Contents

page

Acknowledgements

We would like to thank the following people for their help and support.

Paul Abberley

Pat Avann

Judy Cooper

Jo Eliot

Graham Gibbs

Trevor Habeshaw

Ann Lewis

Joanna Liddle

Eira Makepeace

Val Milman

Gina Rippon

Kathy Warburton

Introduction

The equal opportunities issue is a complex and problematic aspect of life. Examples of injustices – sexism, racism, ageism, classism, as well as discrimination against lesbians and gays and people with disabilities[1] – abound in everyday life but are often denied or ignored or pass unrecognised. Such injustices are a real problem, which will not disappear without action. Education is one area where action can be taken and, since education is a major influence on people's lives, the practice of equal opportunities here will encourage equal opportunities in other situations. Therefore it is vital that teachers foster equal opportunities.

In this book we have tried, rather than giving recipes for social reform or discussing the history or theory of oppression, to suggest practical and relatively simple ways in which teachers can work for equal opportunities on a day to day basis. Each of the 53 items in the book is written to make sense on its own, though they are grouped into chapters which relate to various aspects of teaching and stages of the academic year.

This book is intended for teachers in further and higher education, though it is equally suitable for anyone engaged in the education and training of adults. Teachers in schools, too, will be able to adapt many of the ideas to their own situations. Some items include handouts to be used in exercises. Copyright is waived for these pages and you are encouraged to make copies of them for your students. You will probably want to use an enlarging photocopier, particularly for handouts on which students are expected to write.

1 We are aware that people with disabilities sometimes wish to refer to themselves as 'disabled people' to convey a positive identity. In this book, however, we have opted for the terms 'people with disabilities' and 'students with disabilities' on the grounds that we see our students as people first.

In writing this book we are very much aware of our own limitations as white British middle-class able-bodied heterosexual women. But since we see the gender relationship as representative of all power relationships, we believe that our experience as women has given us some insight into other kinds of discrimination. Some of the items (e.g. items 26 and 41) refer to specific areas of discrimination; most of them, though they may draw their examples from particular areas, have a more general applicability.

Writing this book has helped us to become more aware of discrimination and of ways of dealing with situations in which discrimination is evident. We hope that reading this book will increase your awareness and give you ideas for ways to promote equal opportunities.

Chapter 1

Admissions

1 Advertising

2 Who applies and who is admitted?

3 Target under-represented groups

4 Specialist introductory courses

Advertising 1

If you and your colleagues are committed to equal opportunities, you need to make sure that you advertise the fact in your prospectus and any other publicity material for your course. The material itself should also reflect this commitment. To check this, examine the material and ask the following questions.

- Does the material explicitly encourage applications from all relevant groups in society? For example, 'This department is committed to equal opportunities and welcomes all applicants regardless of gender, social class, ethnic origin . . .'

- Does the material point out any special provision which is made for particular groups, such as crèche facilities for parents with young children, reading arrangements for people with visual impairments, ramps for people reliant on wheelchairs?

- Does the material point out any limits to what you are able to offer? For example, 'Though this site does not have wheelchair access, it is suitable for students with disabilities other than ambulatory. We particularly welcome students with visual impairments'.

- Does the statement of entry requirements make clear any alternative entry routes, e.g. for mature students?

- Do photographs show people from a cross-section of the population?

- Is the language in which the material is written non-discriminatory? (See Chapter 3.)

- Is the material available on tape for people with visual impairments?

If you can answer 'Yes' to all of these questions, then very little needs to be changed. However, as a further check, you could ask members of under-represented groups for their opinions of the material.

If your answer to any of these questions is 'No', then the publicity material may not be attracting all potential applicants. Discuss this with the person responsible for publicity and suggest some alternatives.

Though it may be impossible to evaluate the effectiveness of any changes, they are nevertheless important. For example, the 1995 Warwick University undergraduate prospectus has photographs of female and male students developing a software programme, working with a digital spectrum analyser and visiting a construction site. The hope is that such photographs will help to dispel the view that only men should study computer science and engineering, and encourage applications from women who are in the minority in these areas. Similarly, if there are men on your psychology courses, show them in your photographs of psychology students since men are in a minority on psychology courses; if you want to encourage students of all ethnic origins to train as teachers, show black students on teaching practice. And don't forget to show a range of students in photographs illustrating leisure and sporting activities.

(See also item 42.)

Who applies and who is admitted? 2

Teachers often have expectations of the abilities of particular groups of students. For example, they may expect white applicants to be more able than black applicants or men to be more able than women. If applicants are interviewed these expectations may influence the sorts of questions which are asked and how the answers are interpreted. Ultimately these expectations may affect decisions as to who is offered a place on a course and who is rejected.

The following is a procedure you can use to check whether or not there are any problems of this kind in admissions.

a After you have made all your decisions in a given year, assign the applicants to groups. Obviously you will be restricted to group membership which can be identified from the application form which means that the amount of information which is available will vary from one institution to another. You will probably be able to divide applicants into groups according to the following criteria: gender (male/female); age (under 21/21 and over); ethnic origins (black/white); marital status (married/single/divorced); education (state school/public school); social class; geographic location (based on home address - north/south; rural/urban); country (overseas/UK). In addition you may be able to distinguish between applicants with or without physical or sensory disabilities.

b Within each group identify those applicants who have been accepted and those who have been rejected.

c You will then need to calculate the proportion of applicants who are offered a place, who are rejected and who apply, for each group. An example is given overleaf.

MARITAL STATUS

	Married	Single	Separated	Divorced	Total
Offered place	25 (8%)	267 (89%)	3 (1%)	5 (2%)	300
Rejected	29 (14%)	165 (80%)	1 (<1%)	10 (5%)	205
Total	54 (11%)	432 (86%)	4 (1%)	15 (3%)	505

In this example you can see that, within each group, the proportions being offered a place and being rejected are roughly similar to the proportion of total applications in that group. However, single people are slightly more likely to be accepted than rejected, whereas the reverse is the case for married and divorced applicants. This could occur for many reasons, but might warrant further exploration. For example, are the married and divorced applicants, who will be on average older than the single applicants, being rejected because they are offering inappropriate entry qualifications? If this is the case, you could explore ways in which your department could advise potential applicants about entry requirements at an earlier stage (see item 3) or you could try admitting students on a 'non-standard entry' basis.

Another possible explanation for the discrepancy is that, because of their non-standard entry qualifications, more divorced and married applicants are being interviewed compared to single applicants. You could check this by producing a table similar to the one above but which examines admissions outcomes for students who are interviewed and those who are not. If a greater proportion of the interviewed students, relative to students who are not interviewed, is being rejected you could explore why this is happening. Is it because they have poor interview skills? Does it become apparent in the interview that they would be better suited to a different course? Is it because they are being asked discriminatory questions during the interview (for example, whether a woman applicant intends to have children during the course) and rejected on the basis of their answers? Once you have identified the reason or reasons, you will need to consider ways of improving the situation.

Target under-represented groups 3

There are a number of things you can do if applicants to your course do not reflect the distribution of groups within the general population. However, first you will need to discover if there is a problem. You can do this by comparing the group membership of your applicants (see item 2) with up-to-date population statistics[1]. Then, if there is a discrepancy, you can try to encourage applicants from any groups which are under-represented. This can be done in several ways.

The first is to check your publicity material (see item 1). You also need to examine where the course is advertised, particularly if it is a specialist course. For example, if you want to attract women to computer courses then you need to advertise in publications that women read.

Many institutions contribute posters and leaflets, and even whole stands, to exhibitions which are set up to publicise courses in higher education. You can prepare your publicity material with under-represented groups in mind and feature members of these groups in your photographs and specifically welcome them in your leaflets.

In addition to written publicity and visual exhibitions, most institutions give talks about the courses they offer. These may involve a member of staff visiting a group of potential students, or the potential students visiting the department. In either case, it is not only what the members of staff say, but the groups which they personally represent, which may be influential.

1 You can find relevant statistics in journals, responsible newspapers and publications such as the *Annual Abstract of Statistics* published by the Central Office for Information.

For example, if women are under-represented on the course, try to arrange for a woman to give the talk. If this is impossible because there is no female staff member, arrange for some female students to be available. It is also worthwhile considering whether particular groups of applicants, e.g. women and men, mature students and school-leavers, should be given separate talks.

Another important consideration is which groups you target. For example, if your course does not receive applications from people in working-class families, arrange for visits to be made to schools in predominantly working-class areas. If mature students are under-represented on your course, arrange to talk to local work and leisure groups. If you have very few students with disabilities, visit special schools.

You need to think carefully about the content of the talk. It is important to give prospective students sufficient information to enable them to decide whether or not your course is appropriate for them. And it is important to look openly at the conflicts which may arise for certain groups, for example child care and full-time study for applicants with young children, different cultural expectations for applicants from different ethnic groups.

(See also item 4.)

Specialist introductory courses 4

There may be a number of reasons why the student population on a course does not reflect the actual proportions of different groups of people in the general population (see item 2). In some cases the problem is that particular groups do not perceive the course to be appropriate for them, either in terms of their qualifications, their interests or their future employment. One example is the under-representation of women on technology-related courses such as engineering. Figures produced by the Universities Central Council on Admissions Service show that the number of women admitted to UK undergraduate courses in engineering and technology was 13 per cent in 1994. This is despite there being plenty of women with appropriate entry qualifications

One way to try to increase the number of applicants from the group which is under-represented is to provide members of that group with more information. Within the UK a number of institutions run courses designed to encourage girls and women to consider careers in engineering and science. Details of these courses and other initiatives are described in a booklet produced by the Engineering Council[1]. An example of how this can be done is a course at Oxford Brookes University called *A Taste of Technology - An Experience for Women.*

A Taste of Technology is a four-day residential course for up to 60 sixth form girls run in the Easter holidays before they apply for higher education. It has run yearly since 1991 and the programme organisers specifically target girls studying maths and science at schools within 40 miles radius of Oxford. The course seeks to convey positive images of women working in science, engineering and industry and to provide the experience of projects in a variety of areas including mechanical engineering, electronics, chemical engineering and biochemistry. Over the four days the girls have the opportunity to meet and talk with women engineers and scientists, female engineering students and teaching staff (the majority of whom are however male since women are under-represented as lecturers in higher education and in the sciences in particular[2]. They get involved in projects based at the University and, over two days, gain 'hands-on' experience of an industrial project at a local company.

Questionnaire feedback indicates that *A Taste of Technology* has influenced girls' choice of degree course in the direction of engineering and science based courses. For example, in 1994, of 44 girls who returned questionnaires at the end of the course, 11 had changed their minds and decided to apply to engineering courses and 2 had changed to science based courses. This is an encouraging outcome.

1 *Women into Science and Engineering*, 1994. Available from The Engineering Council, 10 Maltravers Street, London WC2R 3ER

2 In 1994-95 the department of Physics at the University of Exeter had only one female full-time female member of staff.

Chapter 2

Course content

5 Reading lists

6 Written course material

7 Visual course material

8 Let's look at it this way

Reading lists 5

Melvyn Bragg's ITV series, *The Modern World–Ten Great Writers*, screened in 1988, featured 10 writers, nine of whom were men and all of whom were white and European. Try to avoid making the same mistake yourself when selecting authors, whether literary or academic, for your students' reading lists.

It may be that you are of the opinion that the available books by, for example, women writers are not as good as those by men. (Or you may think that books by black writers are not as good as those by white etc.) If this is the case, you can try an experiment. Put one or two women authors on the list and see how your students react. Since male authors convey the male experience, women students should find it easier to relate to a woman writer, and all students may welcome a variation in approach. (If you want to explore their reactions explicitly, you could start a discussion on the relative merits of the different books by asking for a show of hands and then press students to say why they voted for one book rather than another.)

Alternatively, you could give over the compiling of the reading list to your students, see what they come up with and discuss with them the criteria on which their choices were based.

If for some reason you have no control over your reading lists because they are set by an external body or because you have inherited them from a predecessor, you can use any bias you may find as case study material (see item 6).

Written course material 6

It is likely that you and your colleagues will want to ask students to read material which happens to be discriminatory. For example, women students are bound to come across the use of the pronoun 'he' referring to both men and women; lesbians and gays are repeatedly faced with exclusively heterosexual representations of family life and sexual relationships; black people may be presented with derogatory images of their group. If such material is good in other ways you may decide nevertheless to refer to it. However, to ignore the discriminatory nature of such material is to condone it. As a result you need to spend time raising the students' awareness of this aspect of the material as an issue in its own right. A one-hour procedure for doing this is suggested below.

a Select a relevant piece of material from your course. This could be a novel, a journal article, an extract from a set text.

b Identify for yourself beforehand a group discriminated against in the material. It might be women, black people, homosexuals, people with special needs etc.

c Divide the students into two groups representing the group discriminated against and the group not discriminated against (who may represent the group supporting the discrimination). If both groups are not represented divide the students on some other basis, such as women/men.

d Explain to the students that the purpose of the exercise is to get them to be more critical of discriminatory material which they come across in their studies.

e Ask the groups to examine the material for the use of language and images which are discriminatory. They should identify how the discrimination is conveyed. (This should take about 20 minutes depending on the nature of the material.)

f Ask the groups to discuss how they feel about discrimination. Do members of each group feel that they are discriminated against in ways that are portrayed in the material? Do they feel discriminated against in ways other than those portrayed in the material? Do they themselves discriminate against people in the ways portrayed in the material? (This should again take about 20 minutes.)

g Bring the two groups together and ask each group how they feel about the images which are portrayed. (Allow 10 minutes for this.)

h Pool suggestions of alternative language and images which would not be discriminatory. (Allow five minutes for this.)

i Encourage your students to continue to be aware of the use of discriminatory material and to alert their other teachers to its danger.

Visual course material 7

Visual course materials – educational slides, films and videos, text book illustrations and cartoons – can be just as discriminatory as written materials. And studies in the psychology of perception indicate that their impact is likely to be greater.

For example, a health education film on the subject of contraception[1], which clearly includes Asian people in its target audience since it has subtitles in several Asian languages, depicts a bed decorated with hearts, which is a western symbol, and a woman consulting a male doctor, which is antagonistic to Asian cultural traditions.

Check your course materials for discrimination and bring it to the attention of your students. At the same time, make a collection of non-discriminatory illustrations to show them. For example, Adrienne L. Zihlman's *The Human Evolution Coloring Book*[2] has pictures of women and men on alternate pages to illustrate the species 'human' (see page 31), and Desmond Morris's most recent television series was entitled *The Human Zoo*[3], which is an improvement on the title of his earlier series *Manwatching*[4].

Encourage your students to notice discrimination themselves in their course materials. One way in which you can help them to be more critical is to get them to do the following exercise with a biased video.

1 *Happy Family Planning*, Family Planning Association, 1970.

2 Illustrations by Carla Simmons, Wynn Kapit, Fran Milner and Cyndie Clark-Huegel in Adrienne L. Zihlman, *The Human Evolution Coloring Book*, Harper & Row, New York, 1982.

3 Desmond Morris, *The Human Zoo*, BBC 1994.

4 Desmond Morris, *Manwatching*, NBBC, 1980

a Explain to the group that the aim is to identify discriminatory material in the video. Remind them that this may be explicit or implicit, verbal or non-verbal. Tell them that they should call out whenever they see or hear something which strikes them as discriminatory.

b When someone calls out, put the video recorder on 'pause' and ask the student to explain in what way that part of the video is discriminatory and how it could be improved. You can also rewind the tape and play the relevant section again if necessary. Then continue playing.

c When the whole tape has been viewed in this way, you can encourage general discussion and maybe also ask the students to write a report on the video.

(See also item 6.)

Figure 1

Illustration of the species 'human' from Adrienne L. Zihlman's *The Human Evolution Colouring Book*, Harper & Row, New York, 1982.

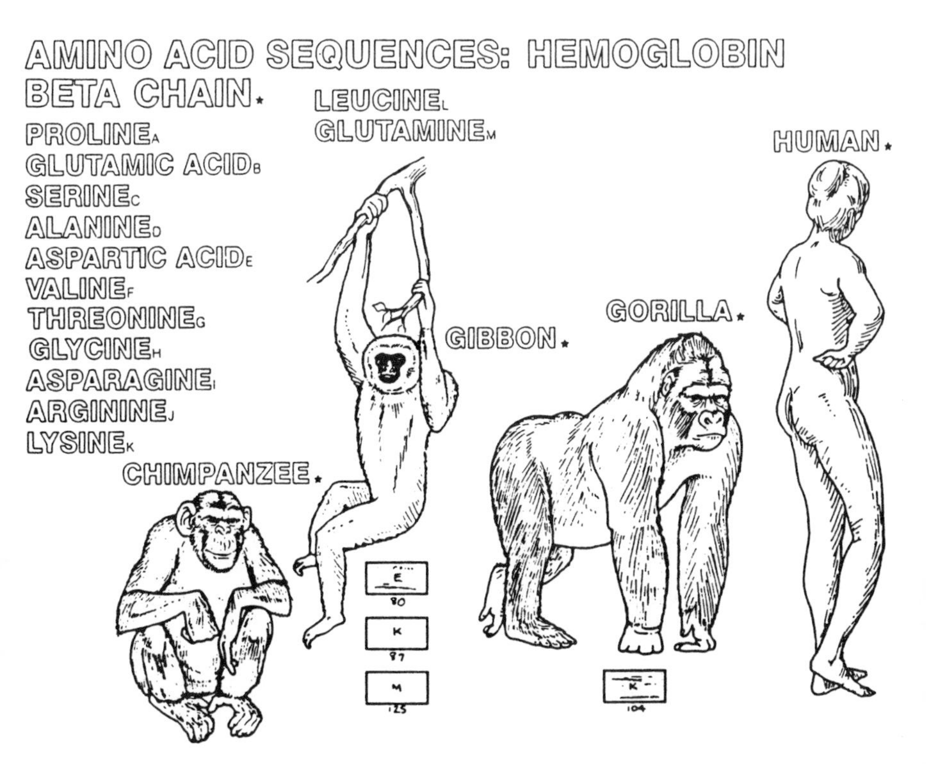

Figure 1

Let's look at it this way 8

Students tend to be taught from the viewpoint of those who hold the power. A consequence of this is that, because the majority of teachers in further and higher education are white, middle-class and male, history is too often concerned with supremacy, science with achievement, physical education with competition, literature with the British tradition etc. Even subjects like sociology and health education, which aim to address the problems of the disadvantaged, run the risk of adopting a patronising approach.

One way to overcome this is to look at your subject from the point of view of an excluded group, e.g. lesbians, gays, socio-economic groups 4 and 5, black people, women. If you or your students are members of such a group, you should find this quite easy. If not, you will need to consult members of the excluded group or their writings and use your imagination. What you decide to do will depend on your syllabus and your preferences and those of your students but you may be able to apply some of the following ideas to your own situation.

- There is a growing body of feminist writing which deals with the exclusion and disempowering of women. This can be applied to any discipline area.

- Discipline areas such as biology, literature, medicine and social work which include topics on sexuality and ageing, for example, can be studied for part of the time from the point of view of lesbians and gays, or old people.

- International subjects such as politics, international relations, geography and history can be studied from the points of view of other nations, especially if there are overseas students in the class.

- Economics students can study monetarism from the point of view of debtor nations or the unemployed.

- In literature there are books which foreground characters who play minor parts in other books. For example, *Wide Sargasso Sea*[1] is about Mr Rochester's mad wife in *Jane Eyre* and *Rosencrantz and Guildenstern are Dead*[2] features two minor and expendable characters from *Hamlet.* Texts such as these can be studied and imitated by students. For example they can rewrite selected passages of set texts in order to foreground characters who have been silenced or undervalued.

1 Jean Rhys, *Wide Sargasso Sea*, Penguin, Harmondsworth, 1966.

2 Tom Stoppard, *Rosencrantz and Guildenstern are Dead*, Faber and Faber, London, 1967.

Chapter 3

Language use

9 Labelling

10 Person-kind language

11 Saying ‘she’

12 Writing ‘she’

13 Acknowledging differences

14 Asking open questions

15 In your own words

Labelling 9

There are many uses of language which place the person designated in an inferior position to the speaker. For example, men may refer to women as 'the girls', 'the ladies', 'members of the fairer sex', 'dumb blondes', 'the weaker sex'; the terms 'dear', 'dearie' or 'love' may be used. Within a profession, a man may refer to a woman as 'the lady psychologist', 'the lady doctor', 'the lady accountant'. Such language is usually spoken but can also occur in the written form such as a woman student being described in a reference as 'this young girl'.

Much of this language is specifically used of women rather than of men, although examples can be found where the person referred to is not necessarily a woman. For example, mature students may be labelled 'the oldies'; less able students 'the thickies'; a small person 'shortie'; homosexuals 'poofs'; students 'kids'; black people 'coloureds'; people with disabilities 'cripples' and so on. When one person speaks in this sort of way to another, the latter person feels inhibited and humiliated. Such language must be avoided.

In rather a different way, particular characteristics of certain groups are sometimes used in a derogatory way to refer to people outside of the group. For example, a teacher may say 'Are you deaf?' or 'Are you blind?' to a student who has misunderstood something or whose attention has wandered in class. Such expressions may make the person to whom they are directed feel uncomfortable, but their use is far more distressing for those who belong to the group whose characteristics are being used as terms of abuse. Such language should also be avoided.

To begin with, write down any examples of derogatory labelling you hear people using in situations such as: staff talking to students; staff talking amongst themselves about students; students talking to one another; senior staff talking about junior staff. Note the context of each example. Monitor your own language.

Try to avoid using such language yourself. You may also like to circulate your list of examples to colleagues who are sympathetic to equal opportunities. As a group you may then feel that you could present it to a staff meeting pointing out why it is important to avoid this sort of language.

You could also present the examples to a general meeting of students.

'Person-kind' language 10

There are many words and phrases in our language which are composites or idioms using 'man'. Some examples are MANpower, MAN-made, to MAN, MAN-size, MAN-hour, MAN-eater, MANfully, MAN-handle, chairMAN, MANkind, MANly, the MAN in the street, to a MAN, MAN Friday, MAN of letters, MAN to MAN, salesMAN, postMAN, craftsMAN, the right MAN, the top MAN. Their use is not restricted to situations which involve just men; all of them can be and are used in contexts involving women and men, separately or collectively. However, their use may contribute to the feeling which many women have of being less important than men. In education this feeling may result in women having lower aspirations than men and underrating their own achievements.

The use of this sort of word or phrase is not usually necessary, since there are alternatives for all of them. For example, those listed above could be replaced as follows:

- MANpower – workforce
- MAN-made – artificial
- to MAN – to run, to staff
- MAN-size – large
- MAN-hour – work hour
- MAN-eater – cannibal
- MANfully – vigorously, bravely
- MAN-handle – handle roughly

- chairMAN – chairperson, chair, convener
- MANkind – the human race
- MANly – brave, dignified
- the MAN in the street – the ordinary person
- to a MAN – without exception
- MAN Friday – factotum
- MAN of letters – scholar, writer
- MAN to MAN – frank and confidential
- salesMAN – salesperson/sales assistant
- postMAN – postal worker
- craftsMAN – craftsperson/craftsworker
- the right MAN – the right person
- the top MAN – the person at the top

Monitor the written and spoken language around you (both your own and others') for the use of words and phrases incorporating 'man'. Compile a list of these words and find alternatives for each of them. Try to use the alternatives in your own language.

As a way of raising awareness of this issue, you could carry out the following exercise.

a Give the list of words and phrases using 'man' to a group of students or colleagues.

b Ask each member of the group to write down alternatives.

c Ask pairs of participants to compare lists.

d Draw up on an acetate or flipchart sheet a full list of alternatives based on participants' suggestions.

e Discuss with the group the relative merits of both sets of words.

f Discuss with the group how you and they can discourage the misuse of 'man' by others.

Saying 'she' 11

In teaching, 'he' is likely to be heard in any situation where the speaker is referring to women and men collectively. However, although the intention in using 'he' may be to refer to both women and men, or girls and boys, the use of 'he' may be interpreted by others as only referring to males. Also, even though we may all know that the use of 'he' is only a convention and doesn't exclude the female gender, it can create feelings in women of being excluded. This may reduce the confidence and aspirations of girls and women. For these reasons it is important to question the exclusive use of 'he'. In addition, there is also a convention that when both gender pronouns are used, 'he' precedes 'she', as in 'he and she'. This also occurs in the case of nouns when both genders are specified, e.g. 'men and women', 'kings and queens', 'host and hostess', 'Jack and Jill', 'Mr and Mrs Smith', 'gays and lesbians'. The order here should also be questioned.

As a start, monitor your own spoken language for your use of the two gender pronouns and the order in which you use them. You could do this in a variety of ways, some of which are listed below.

- Ask a sympathetic colleague to point out every time you use the pronouns 'she' and 'he' inappropriately.

- Audio-record a lecture or seminar or other teaching situation and identify any use of 'she' and of 'he' in the recording.

- Tell your students what you are doing and ask them to tell you whenever you use 'she' or 'he' inappropriately.

Having monitored your own language, you might like to consider some of the following questions.

- Do you use 'he' to refer to both genders?
- Do you ever use 'he and she'?
- Do you ever use 'she and he'?
- In what situations (if any) do you use 'she'?
- Do you ever use 'she' to refer to both genders?

To change pronoun use, first of all try to use 'he or she' whenever you are referring to both women and men, girls and boys. At this point you will probably need to keep monitoring your spoken language in one of the ways suggested above as a check on yourself. As you become more comfortable with this usage, try reversing the order to 'she or he'. Finally, you might like to try just using 'she' when referring to both women and men, girls and boys. The use of 'she' to refer to both sexes highlights the monopoly that the male pronoun normally has.

Also try to reverse the order of the genders in the case of nouns, saying instead, for example, 'women and men', 'Jane and John Smith', 'Mrs and Mr Jones' and 'lesbians and gays'. This will highlight the precedence usually given to the male in the ordering of the genders.

Writing 'she' 12

In written, as in spoken, language it is common for people to use the pronoun 'he' when they are meaning to refer to both women and men. This can be alienating for women. Although the writer may intend the pronoun 'he' to refer to both women and men, or girls and boys, some readers may interpret the use of 'he' as only referring to males. In addition, the use of 'he' can make it difficult for women to relate to what has been written, despite their knowing that by using 'he' the writer is only following a convention. This may make girls and women feel that the text is not relevant to them. It is therefore important to question the exclusive use of 'he' in written material.

As a start, make a list of all instances you meet in written material when 'he' is used to refer to both women and men. Also notice whether 'she' is ever used to refer to both sexes. You could do this for different types of material, some of which are listed below:

- text books and journal articles
- the prospectus of your institution
- institutional notices
- department notices
- your own writing

There is obviously nothing you can do to change this use of 'he' in published text books and journal articles (although see item 6). However, if 'he' is used exclusively in the prospectus or in institutional and departmental notices you could bring this to the attention of the relevant people, pointing out why the use of 'he' to refer to women and men is undesirable. In your own writing use 'he or she', or 'she or he' when the people referred to are both female and male.

Acknowledging differences 13

There often appears to be confusion about precisely when language discriminates. For example, should we point out differences between people such as their age, their gender, their ethnic origin, or should we ignore these characteristics? One reason for the confusion seems to be linguistic. We describe people who make derogatory remarks about individuals from particular age, gender or ethnic groups as being ageist, sexist or racist. However a myth seems to have developed that to say anything which identifies individuals as members of particular groups, whether derogatory or not, discriminates. Individuals differ from one another in many ways, including their group membership, and acknowledging these differences, provided that they are not ascribed negative values, is often important and relevant.

As an exercise, compare your own language use with the following list of DOs and DON'Ts.

- DON'T make derogatory remarks about people from other groups.

- DO focus on the characteristics of individuals.

- DO address individuals by name. Allow time, on the first occasion that you meet a group, for everyone to learn everyone else's name. Persevere with names that you find difficult, particularly those which sound foreign to you, so that you can all learn to pronounce one another's names correctly and to address one another without hesitation.

- DON'T generalise apparent group characteristics to individual members of the group (e.g. don't ask a black student in a seminar what black people think about the topic under discussion).

- DO identify the ethnic origins of different people when it is relevant to do so (e.g. when you are genuinely interested in hearing about their background or when you know that they have particular experience which the group can benefit from hearing about).

- DO use the words racism, sexism, ageism etc. when appropriate (e.g. when you want to confront people about their behaviour).

As a further exercise, identify some more DOs and DON'Ts associated with acknowledging differences between people. Send your suggestions to us!

Asking open questions 14

In schools, teachers tend to ask boys open questions. For example, 'Why do you think mixing blue and yellow paint makes green?' This sort of question encourages the child to think about the issues involved since the answer is not straightforward. In contrast teachers tend to ask girls closed questions, such as 'What colour do you get when you mix blue and yellow paint?' As a result of the use of different types of question, boys get more opportunity to develop their ideas than girls. This also helps to explain why boys spend more time than girls talking in the classroom.

In order to discover whether you ask men and women different sorts of questions audio-record a seminar. Identify all the questions you ask and categorise them into open and closed questions. Can you identify any pattern to your questioning? Do you direct one sort of question more at male students than at female students? Do you ask members of other groups predominantly one type of question?

If you discover that you have a tendency to put closed questions to some groups and open questions to others, you could try to eliminate this by only asking open questions. Since this type of question is likely to encourage the students to think about the topic, it is in any case the appropriate form for education.

In your own words 15

Students are often criticised and corrected for speaking or writing in a way which is considered unacceptable, even when the language they use – such as West Indian patois, colloquial or regional English or subjective or dated language – is just as complex, rich and expressive as standard English. Once again the white, male, middle-class students are being rewarded simply for being white, male and middle-class.

It is a central aim of education that students extend their vocabulary and linguistic competence and learn the particular language of the subjects they are studying, but this should never be at the expense of denying their own way of expressing themselves.

If you respect your students' own ways of expressing themselves and give them the opportunity to explore ideas in a language they feel comfortable with, this will not only counter discrimination in the classroom but also give them a good basis from which to develop linguistic competence in their subject area. It will also, incidentally, enable you to judge whether they have really understood a topic if they don't just repeat the words of the text book.

Students will usually need encouragement before they will risk using their own words. The following examples are suggestions of specific ways in which you may be able to offer them that encouragement.

- Ask them what different kinds of English they speak and how comfortable they feel with each.

- Prompt them by saying 'How would you explain/describe/argue that point in your own words?'

- Set them writing tasks in informal modes such as letters or dialogues.

- Show them that you value differences by asking 'How many different ways of saying that can we think of as a group?'

- Don't comment on the way they express themselves until they have built up enough confidence to ask for feedback themselves.

- Look for examples in your discipline area of language being used in new and flexible ways and show them to your students.

There will generally be more opportunity in social studies and arts subjects for students to be encouraged to use their own words. However, the methods suggested above can also be used in science subjects. For example, a laboratory report can be written in the form of a letter to someone known to the student who is unfamiliar with the subject and scientific debates can be written in dialogue form. Or you could set your students essay titles beginning 'In your own words . . . '

Chapter 4

Teaching methods

What's funny? 16

Everyone likes to make and to hear jokes. They provide an opportunity for laughter and can be used to break up the contents of a lecture. However, many jokes make fun of particular groups of the population, by ascribing them derogatory characteristics. Such jokes should not be made. They are not amusing for anyone who belongs to the group, often a minority group, at whose expense the joke is made. They are not amusing to people who are concerned with eliminating discrimination.

Monitor the content of the jokes you make and the jokes you hear. Refrain from using in your lectures and seminars (and everyday life) any jokes which do discriminate.

(See also item 48.)

Sitting in a circle 17

Many teaching situations consist of a teacher at the front of a class. There may be a desk or lectern which faces the class and it may even be on a raised platform. Chairs for the students are often placed in ordered rows facing the teacher. This physical arrangement provides a clear division between the teacher and the students and is based on the assumption that one person, the teacher, will be in control. This can accentuate the inequality in power which exists between you and your students. In some situations this may be desirable, for example if essential information, which only the teacher has, is being given to the students. However, it is particularly undesirable in seminars when students should have the opportunity to discuss their ideas with a teacher, criticise the teacher's contribution, and communicate with one another. A difference in power between the students and the teacher can lead to the situation in which a seminar turns into a lecture, with the teacher talking all the time and no students contributing. Alternatively it may result in a situation in which some of the students, e.g. white males, feel more able than the others to contribute.

By changing the seating arrangements in a seminar room it is possible to reduce some of the power differences, although obviously the teacher will still have more power than the students. Move the tables to the edge of the room and arrange the chairs in a circle in the space which is left. Make sure that the chairs are equidistant from one another, and if the chair that was behind the teacher's desk is different, remove it or make sure that you don't sit in it. Avoid sitting in the chair nearest the board. Your aim is to create a physical setup such that an onlooker would not be able to tell you apart from the students.

Everyone contributes 18

Some students may talk at length in seminars, while others may not say anything at all. There are many reasons why some students do not speak: they may feel that they have nothing to contribute; they may feel in awe of the teacher and of the other students or they may belong to a group (e.g. female) which is often silent. This can lead to the situation in which one or two students monopolise the seminar. Because of their previous experiences these are often white middle-class men.

This situation can be altered by introducing some ground rules at the beginning of a seminar, and nominating someone to check that they are complied with (see item 34). Three possible ground rules are suggested below.

- No-one is allowed to make two points in succession.
- No-one is allowed to talk for more than one minute.
- No-one is allowed to speak for a second time until everyone has spoken once.

As an alternative to specifying these ground rules, you could suggest a round. A round is when everyone in turn, including you, makes a statement, uninterrupted, on a particular topic. There are specific ground rules for rounds.

- Speak in turn, not out of turn.
- It's OK to pass.

- It's OK to repeat what someone else has said already.[1]

You could ask each person in turn to say something at the beginning, middle and end of the seminar. This would ensure that everyone has three opportunities to talk.

- The first round at the beginning of the seminar could be either 'Something I find difficult about this topic' or 'Something I find interesting about this topic'.

- The round in the middle of the seminar could be either 'Something about this topic that I'm still confused about' or 'Something about this topic that I'd like to talk about some more'.

- The final round at the end of the seminar could be either 'Something I've enjoyed about this seminar' or 'Something I've learned from listening to other people'.

This is especially valuable in the first year, at the start of a new year or at the first meeting of a new group as it accustoms group members to the expectation that everyone should contribute.

[1] Sue Habeshaw, Trevor Habeshaw and Graham Gibbs, Item 22 in *53 Interesting Things to Do in Your Seminars and Tutorials*, Technical and Educational Services Ltd., Bristol, 4th edition, 1992.

Everyone brings something 19

As the teacher, you have much more influence over what is taught than your students. You will decide on the content of the lectures, and normally seminars will relate to a preceding lecture or to reading suggested by you. Students are reluctant to stray from material you have recommended.

One way to increase your students' influence is to invite them to bring to seminars material they have discovered for themselves. At least two days before a seminar tell the students the topic to be discussed. Ask them to look at recent additions to the library, i.e. new books or journal articles, and select a point of interest or a relevant article. If the topic is of current national interest, you could also ask them to bring cuttings from daily newspapers, tabloids as well as 'quality' papers. They should each come to the seminar prepared to give a brief résumé of what they have found and say how it relates to the topic under discussion. Divide up the available time so that there is at least 10 minutes left at the end for any general points of discussion. If the group is large, you can ask the students to exchange their finds in groups of four, and ask each group of four to report back briefly to the main group before the end of the seminar.

This teaching method not only reduces the disparity of power between teacher and students but also fosters equality among students, since all of the students are asked to bring something and they all have the same amount of time in which to tell the others about their contribution.

Pyramid 20

There is clear evidence that in schools boys occupy more of the teachers' time than girls. One reason for this is that boys make more spoken contributions than girls. It seems likely that this difference will persist into further and higher education. In seminars this may result in the men dominating the discussion, with the women contributing less. Of course, there may be other reasons such as age, nationality etc. why some students contribute more than others. One way to reduce this effect is to make sure that everyone has the opportunity to talk to at least one other person in the seminar. This can be achieved as follows.

Set a question for the seminar, giving the students prior warning. Before the seminar identify two questions which lead up to the set question. An example is given below.

- Set question Can studies of children with motor difficulties help to elucidate the role of action in development?
- Question 1 What are the key features of theories of development which give a role to action?
- Question 2 How does the development of children with motor difficulties whom you have known or read about differ from children without motor difficulties?

After introducing the seminar, take the group through the stages which follow. Suggestions for timing are given in brackets.

Stage 1: Individuals (5 minutes)

Students write down notes of their own in response to Question 1.

Stage 2: Pairs (10 minutes)

Pairs of students share what they have written and, after doing this, consider question 2.

Stage 3: Fours (20 minutes)

Pairs join together to make fours and share their answers to question 2 and consider points they would raise in response to the set question.

Stage 4: Plenary (15 minutes)

For the remainder of the seminar each group of four reports on the points that arose in their group. Ask a representative from each group to contribute one point at a time, before moving on to the next group. Continue this process round the groups until all the points have been exhausted.

Student-only seminars 21

Seminars are not supposed to be lectures. Unfortunately, because you hold a more powerful position than your students they may expect you to lead the seminar and do most of the talking. Students vary, because of age, gender, nationality etc., in the extent to which this power difference inhibits them but some of them may feel unable to say anything in front of you. This difficulty can be reduced by leaving the students to work on their own.

If you decide to do this it is important that you discuss with the students why you are going to leave them and make sure that they are happy about this. It is also important that you agree with the students at the beginning of the seminar what they are going to do while you are away. You should also be available for them to contact you during your absence if they want to.

If the seminar is 50 minutes long, spend up to the first 10 minutes with the students, agreeing what they are going to do. When you first try this, students may only want to be left for 10 or 15 minutes, but as they become more experienced they may ask to be left for 30 minutes. Make sure that you return for at least 10 minutes at the end. In this time the students can summarise what has happened in your absence, and turn to you for clarification of any queries which they have been unable to resolve themselves.

Open-book seminars 22

Seminars should provide the opportunity for students to work through ideas and issues which have been raised in other parts of their course or in their reading. However, students often feel inferior in the presence of a teacher, who, they suppose, has all the answers. They may also feel inferior to some of the other students. Inequality in knowledge is, to an extent, an inevitable part of education; however it can be detrimental to learning. It can result in some students keeping quiet in a seminar and failing to admit when they can't remember something. It can result in some students not turning up to seminars because they get so little out of them. A consequence of this is that the teacher and one or two students may do most of the talking.

Encourage students to bring books and notes to seminars. Make it clear to them that you do not expect them to remember all that they have read, and give them the opportunity within the seminar to look up information when they need to. This, used in conjunction with the suggestions in items 20 and 21, can be extremely effective.

Chapter 5

Marking

Alternative assessment procedures 23

The experience of education is different for everyone. One aspect of this is that individuals differ in how they can best show what they have learned. Some people find it easier to give a spoken answer to a question; others prefer to write it down. Some find unseen examinations extremely stressful. The same people may be far less stressed if they are given the questions some time before the examination. For some, writing essays for assessment is preferable to sitting examinations. Some work better if they have plenty of time, whereas others work to good effect when they have limited time.

If you want to make your course as equitable as possible, then you need to think carefully about the assessment procedures you use. Are they fair for everyone? To begin with, ask yourself what variety and choice students have. If you have a single assessment procedure, for example an unseen examination, it is unlikely that this will give all of your students the same opportunity to demonstrate what they know and understand. If you already have a range of procedures, then you may like to consider the possibility of introducing some more.

There are usually some institutional constraints on how you can assess your students: for example, at Warwick University at least 50 per cent of each student's final marks must come from unseen examinations. There are however numerous ways in which this can be achieved: every course whose marks contribute to the final degree could be assessed half on essays, half on unseen examinations; half of the courses could be assessed entirely by unseen examinations, the rest by essays; some courses could be assessed by essays written and handed in throughout the course, others by essays handed in at the end of the course; a proportion of the non-examination marks could come from an oral presentation of a piece of work. In some cases – for example, on a modular course assessing some components by unseen examinations, others by essays – you may be able to let the students choose.

If you set examination questions and essay titles for the courses you teach, then here you can provide choice for your students. Try to ask a variety of types of question which may appeal to different students. (Examples of different ways of asking questions can be found in *53 Interesting Ways to Assess Your Students*[1].) You could also consider giving your students the opportunity of negotiating their own essay titles with you.

When you introduce choice for your students in how they are assessed it is important that you give them as much feedback as possible on how they perform. If, for example, a student finds exams very stressful but nevertheless does well in them, she or he needs this information in order to make the right choice between assessment by essays or by examination.

1 Graham Gibbs, Sue Habeshaw and Trevor Habeshaw, *53 Interesting Ways to Assess Your Students*, Technical and Educational Services Ltd., Bristol, 3rd edition, 1993.

Rewriting questions 24

Certain ways in which examination or essay questions are phrased may put some students at a disadvantage. For example, the use of 'man's' in the following question may alienate women students.

- Question 'Outline ways in which man's brain differs from those of other higher primates.'

In addition, it could be argued that this particular question is ambiguous, since it could be interpreted as requiring a comparison between the brains of men and women, rather than between the human brain and the brains of primates lower down the evolutionary scale.

Other questions may reflect assumptions which are discriminatory. The first of the following questions makes the assumption that black people are inferior to white people; the second question assumes that only men write books.

- Question 'Can blacks ever achieve the same educational standard as whites?'

- Question 'Discuss the view that the author constructs not only his characters but also his readers.'

If questions are to be fair to all the candidates it is imperative that they are designed in such a way that all possible bias is avoided. The above three questions could be rephrased in the following way.

- Question 'Outline ways in which the human brain differs from those of other higher primates.'

- Question 'Critically discuss the evidence which has been interpreted to suggest that black people may be less able than white people.'

- Question 'Discuss the view that authors construct not only their characters but also their readers.'

Take a careful look at past questions which you have set. Can you detect any bias? Give the questions to a group of students and ask them if they can. Try to rephrase any questions which are biased.

Giving feedback to students 25

Your students may unintentionally use discriminatory language in their essays. For example, they may use 'coloured people' when they are meaning to refer to black people or 'mother' when they are meaning to refer to either parent; they may adopt a Eurocentric or patriarchal stance; they may make assumptions about what members of particular groups can or can't do. You can bring this to their attention in your feedback when you mark their essays. However, it is important that you tell your students before they start writing their essays that you intend to pay attention to their language use.

When you identify a discriminatory use of words point out to the student why you feel that it is discriminatory. You could suggest alternative forms of words. After you have given some examples to the student suggest that she or he tries to rewrite any passages which do discriminate.

Students with writing difficulties 26

Much assessment in education at all levels is assessment of written work. Many degrees in particular could be said to be degrees in writing. This means that a difficulty which prevents a student reaching her or his potential in written work has particularly serious implications. Some difficulties are obvious. These include visual impairment, and injuries and disabilities of the hand or arm. These may require some form of special provision which your institution will almost certainly provide if requested to do so. Other difficulties are much less easily recognised. For example, students with impaired hearing and students who use non-standard English may have difficulties writing in ways which are expected of students in higher education. One of the most common difficulties and often the least recognised is dyslexia.

For suggestions of ways of helping students who use a non-standard form of English see item 15. However, if your students have writing difficulties as a result of some disability there are several ways in which you can help. First it is important to establish the case. Ask any students concerned to provide evidence and details of their condition and their needs. For example, if they may be dyslexic, ask them to arrange to be assessed. There are centres throughout the country and you can get your local address from The British Dyslexia Institute, 98 London Road, Reading, RG1 5AU (telephone 01734 668271).

Though there is a charge for the assessment, students in receipt of a local authority grant can apply for financial assistance in paying the fee. They may also be eligible for other allowances: substantial sums are available to students with dyslexia on local authority grants to enable them to buy word processors, tape recorders or other equipment or to pay for non-medical help. Information about these grants can be obtained from the student's grant-awarding authority or from the Students' Union welfare section or from the institution's student services unit.

Provided you have supporting evidence you should find it easy to persuade your students' examiners, whether internal or external, to make special arrangements for students with recognised writing disabilities. These arrangements could consist of one or more of the following:

- oral exams
- special weightings for course work and contributions to group discussions
- a time allowance in written exams, e.g. 15 minutes extra for every hour of the exam
- an agreed percentage to be added to the student's papers by way of compensation
- a separate examination room and the use of a tape recorder or the services of an amanuensis (the Students' Union will sometimes be able to help by providing an amanuensis) though suitable rehearsal beforehand is also necessary if the student is to be able to dictate coherently
- a separate examination room with an invigilator authorised to give the student help with spelling
- an extended course (The British Dyslexia Institute suggests that some students with dyslexia may benefit if they take four years over an undergraduate course instead of the customary three.)
- use of a computer for word processing the exam answers

Once a procedure has been established it is a good idea to get the examiners to agree that it constitutes a precedent so that other students in the future can benefit from it.

Anonymous marking 27

A teacher's intention, when marking either an essay for assessment or an unseen examination answer, should be to give marks for what has been written. However, there is clear evidence that examination scripts ascribed to women are more likely to be given marks in the middle of the range (i.e. 2:2's) than are scripts ascribed to men, and that the latter are more likely to be given marks towards the extremes of the scale (i.e. 1st's and 3rd's). When information about gender is removed from examination scripts the different distributions of marks for men and women disappear.

The marker will be aware of gender if the full names of the students are written on the scripts. Full names may also provide information about ethnic groups, which may influence the marks awarded if the marker has different expectations of the ability of members of different races.

If marks are to reflect only the quality of the piece of work, the name of the person who wrote it must be concealed from the marker. This can be achieved by using the following procedure, which is in operation in a number of universities in the UK.

a The institution assigns each student a unique number at the beginning of the course. Student Registration numbers can be used.

b A record of names and numbers is kept centrally for decoding after the marks have been given.

c The student puts her or his number, but not her or his name, on all pieces of assessed work and on exam scripts.

d The work is marked.

e When all the student's work has been marked and an overall mark has been agreed, the student's identity is revealed.

f Any circumstances, such as illness, which may have influenced the student's mark can then be discussed.

If your institution does not operate an anonymous marking system you should propose, through appropriate channels, that it does (see item 53).

However, if for some reason your institution refuses to implement such a procedure, you could use one of the following ideas.

- Suggest to your students that they submit their work with just the initials of their given names. Although you will know who they are and therefore know their gender, this information will not be available to external examiners (nor to second markers unless they too know the students).

- If the students write their exam answers in booklets, such that all the details of the candidate are on the front cover, you can fold back the covers of all the booklets before you start marking. When you have decided on a mark for a script, write it down and only then look to the front cover to identify the candidate. Under no circumstances change your mark!

- Arrange for a pair of small sticky labels to be printed for each student. Each label should bear a number which is unique to the student, and one of the labels should also bear the student's name. A list of the name/number pairings should be made. The name/number label is stuck onto the front cover of the examination booklet close to where the student has written her/his name and the second label, bearing the student's number, is stuck elsewhere on the booklet. The part of the booklet bearing the student's name and name/number label is then torn off and kept safely. (Ideally this process should be carried out by someone not involved with the marking of the papers.)

Chapter 6

Equal opportunities exercises

Ever been harassed? 28

Teachers often behave in ways which make students feel uncomfortable. For example, a teacher may use familiar terms, such as 'love' and 'dear', when addressing individual students; a teacher may wink at a student, sit very close to or touch a student; a teacher may comment on a student's personal dress or lifestyle; a teacher may make jokes about members of particular groups. The teacher may be completely unaware that this behaviour is causing any distress, and may even think it is friendly and amusing. Because of differences in status between the teacher and the students it is usually difficult for students to tell the member of staff concerned, or anyone else, how they feel. These sorts of difficulties are not confined to teacher/student relationships; they may also arise between students and between members of staff.

The following exercise is a way of raising staff and students' awareness of how recipients feel about this sort of behaviour.

a Choose a group to run the exercise with. Possible groups would be women, black people or gays. You should only offer the exercise to people from groups to which you also belong, e.g. a woman should run the exercise with women. This is because the exercise requires people to share very personal feelings about how others, outside their group, behave towards them. The presence of a non-member could be very threatening.

b At the outset you need to explain the purpose of the exercise.

- To give the participants the opportunity to talk about difficult and embarrassing situations which they have experienced and which have arisen because they belong to a particular group.

- To produce a list of remarks or behaviours which have caused distress, and to present this to members of the group which has behaved in this way. It is important here to assure participants of complete confidentiality: neither the originators nor the recipients of the behaviours will be identified on the list, nor mentioned to anyone outside of the group.

- To inform participants of any procedures through which they can formally make complaints about other people's behaviour, if they wish to, and of any counselling or support groups they may wish to join.

c Give everyone five minutes on their own to think about things which have been said or done to them which they have found upsetting or embarrassing. Everyone should write down their examples.

d Ask everyone, in pairs, to share their examples, describing the circumstances, what happened, how they felt and what, if anything, they did. Allow 10 minutes for this, plus a further five minutes if necessary.

e Ask everyone in the group to contribute examples which will be shown, without names attached, to people outside the group. Make two separate lists, of verbal and non-verbal behaviour.

f Tell the students about any procedures for dealing with harassment which exist in your institution.

g Tell the students about any support services which are available.

h After the meeting make copies of the lists for everyone in the group.

i Present the lists to a meeting of your department or course team as a way of opening discussion on the issue of harassment. This can be more effective if, in the meeting with students, you ask them to distinguish between harassment by members of staff and harassment by other students. At the staff meeting you could then present the staff examples. Be prepared for opposition, denial and complete lack of understanding of why the behaviour should cause offence. (If possible obtain the support of one or two sympathetic colleagues before the start of the meeting.)

j If no procedures for dealing with harassment exist in your institution, you could propose the formation of a working party with the brief to draft an equal opportunities policy (see item 53).

Exercises in rewriting 29

In an *Everyman* film (broadcast in 1988) featuring the ordination of women in the Anglican Church, a group campaigning in Australia sang a rewritten version of Bunyan's 'He who would valiant be':

> She who would valiant be
> 'Gainst all disaster,
> Let her in constancy
> Follow the Master.
> There's no discouragement
> Shall make her once relent
> Her first avowed intent
> To be a pilgrim . . .

A simple way of raising gender awareness is to select a passage which is strongly biased towards either male or female and get your students to rewrite it by changing the gender of the personal pronouns.

For example, people are accustomed to accepting the gender stereotyping of popular romance. You can challenge this by asking your students to rewrite the following passage, substituting Simon for Sabina and reversing 'he' and 'she', 'him' and 'her' and 'man' and 'woman'. Or you can ask them to rewrite it, substituting 'he' for 'she' etc. but retaining Sabina and the female pronouns, so that the passage reads as a lesbian love scene.

> 'I've always had a weakness for blondes.'
>
> Once again his head lowered and he claimed her lips, gently this time , parting them persuasively as he deepened the kiss.
>
> In that moment everything in Sabina's life suddenly changed, became more ordered. A stranger, a cold hard man embittered by she didn't know

> what, was making her his with a touch of his lips and hands, was arousing her as never before, and she couldn't possibly marry anyone else but him. Her body arched against his, her curves fitting perfectly against the hardness of his body, her hands going up to his shoulders and tangling in the thick blackness of his hair as she strained him closer to her
>
> Carole Mortimer, *Satan's Master*, Mills and Boon, 1981

As well as causing a lot of hilarity, an exercise of this kind forces people to face their assumptions and stereotypes.

There are clear opportunities for rewriting exercises, not only on courses in literature and popular culture but on other courses too. Look out for passages in your own area which are heavily biased; for example, the writer may assume that all nurses are female, all legal clients are male etc. The use in all subject areas of 'mankind' and 'man' to mean human beings can be challenged too; students can be encouraged to find ways of rewriting such passages to cover both genders.

Exercises of this kind are not generally complete in themselves; students and staff need time to reflect on the experience and talk about it. This can be done in pairs or small groups or in a plenary session with the whole class if numbers are not too big.

For additional exercises which include rewriting, see items 6, 8, 10, 24 and 25.

Exercises in sentence completion 30

Assumptions about the characteristics of particular groups must always be questioned. Such assumptions are generally unfounded and lead to the stereotyping of members of those groups, causing them distress.

One way of questioning such assumptions is the use of sentence completion exercises. This type of exercise usually works well because participants, given the beginning of the sentence, will often complete it without realising until later the implications of what they have written. This can give them useful insights into their attitudes.

Two exercises which could be used with groups of students are described below. They are particularly useful where you want to challenge stereotypical views which you believe to be held by the group.

Exercise 1

Before the meeting:

a Select one issue you want to work on with your students. Possible examples include gender, ethnic origin, class, marital status, disability, sexual orientation, age, size.

b Draw up pairs of unfinished sentences of the following form.

  i As a female I must . . .
  As a male I could . . .

  ii As a male I must . . .
  As a female I could . . .

c Photocopy pairs of statements so that (for this example) all the women can have a copy of i and all the men have a copy of ii.

At the meeting:

a Give each student the appropriate pair of statements and allow them two minutes to fill in their responses.

b Divide the group into two on the basis of the issue involved: for the example used here, into groups of women and men.

c Ask each group, using their individual responses, to draw up a list of things they feel they must do as a member of their own group, and a list of things they feel they could do as a member of the other group. (Allow 10 minutes for this.)

d Exchange lists between the groups. Give the groups 10 minutes to discuss the content of each other's lists.

e Bring the groups together. Use the following questions to guide discussion.

- What do you notice about the two lists?

- Do all members of each group share any characteristics (apart from their gender)?

- Does either group assume characteristics for the other? Are these characteristics justified?

- What does this exercise demonstrate about assumptions?

Exercise 2

Before the meeting:

a Draw up a list of 20 unfinished sentences of the following form.

- Elderly people need . . .
- Black people are . . .
- Being a student means . . .
- Women should . . .
- Working-class people should not . . .
- People with disabilities can . . .

Your list of statements could cover any issue you want to raise. Possible examples include gender, ethnic origin, class, marital status, disability, sexual orientation, age, size.

b Photocopy the list of statements so that everyone in the group can have a copy.

At the meeting:

a Give a copy of the list to each student and allow them five minutes to complete the sentences.

b Ask pairs of students to compare responses.

c Draw up a list of responses made to each statement.

d Guide discussion of the list by considering, for each statement in turn, whether all of the responses are true for all members of the group identified. Do all members of any group share any characteristics? What are these?

e Encourage students to assess the implications of the conclusions they draw.

Other things being equal 31

Stereotyping of individuals on the basis of their membership of a particular group leads to a whole range of false expectations about their characteristics, abilities and behaviour. The following exercise provides the opportunity for you to discuss with your students the dangers of stereotyping people solely on the basis of their group membership.

The exercise involves the students discussing the career options and projected futures of two imaginary students, based on written profiles. Half of the group discusses one student, the rest discuss a second student. The two profiles are identical in all ways except one. In the example given below the only difference between the profiles is the gender of the student: one is female and called Jane; the other is male and called John. You could create other profiles in which the students differ from each other in, for example, ethnic origin (in which case you could call the students John and Abdul), class or age, though the profiles should only differ in a single respect.

a Divide your students into two groups. If at all possible arrange for the two groups to work in separate rooms. If this is not feasible, arrange for them to work in opposite corners of the room. Distribute the handouts: give each person in one group a copy of Jane's profile; give each person in the other group a copy of John's profile. Neither group should know that the other group has a different profile, nor how the profiles differ.

  In the first five minutes everyone should read their profile and write down their responses to the questions.

b Ask the members of each group to share their responses with other members of the same group. Allow 10 minutes for this. Someone in each group should make a list of the responses (see item 34). Tell the students that the two groups will exchange lists at the end of the 10 minutes, so they need to write legibly.

c The two groups swop lists. At this point tell the students how the profiles differed. Give the groups time to digest each other's lists.

d Open up discussion by identifying any differences between the two lists. What are the differences? Do they relate to stereotyped views of men and women? Is there any justification for the differences? What are the dangers of stereotyping individuals?

Handout: Jane's profile

Jane is 19. She is taking a humanities degree at a new university. She has been working fairly hard and should get a good lower second class degree, possibly an upper second. She is reasonably outgoing and enthusiastic. Outside of her degree work she has been involved in several community projects and in her vacations she has had various jobs: in a bar, fruit picking, on the assembly line of an engineering firm. She has a supportive family and seems to get on well with people in general.

Imagine that you are the careers officer at Jane's university. Jane has come to see you. What careers advice would you give her?

Imagine Jane in six years' time, at the age of 25. What would you expect her to be doing? Imagine her in 15 years' time, at the age of 34. What would you expect her to be doing?

Handout: John's profile

John is 19. He is taking a humanities degree at a new university. He has been working fairly hard and should get a good lower second class degree, possibly an upper second. He is reasonably outgoing and enthusiastic. Outside of his degree work he has been involved in several community projects and in his vacations he has had various jobs: in a bar, fruit picking, on the assembly line of an engineering firm. He has a supportive family and seems to get on well with people in general.

Imagine that you are the careers officer at John's university. John has come to see you. What careers advice would you give him?

Imagine John in six years' time, at the age of 25. What would you expect him to be doing? Imagine him in 15 years' time, at the age of 34. What would you expect him to be doing?

Group relations exercise 32

Students – and teachers – can easily fall into a routine of giving pat answers to questions of equal opportunities. This exercise is designed to give them a reminder of some of the real experiences of discrimination, but in a safe situation and with the opportunity to reflect on the meaning of the experience. By working in separate groups, the students demonstrate for themselves ways in which groups tend to exaggerate differences between them and stereotype each other.

a Explain to your students that the purpose of the exercise is to get a feel of discrimination and to see what they can learn from it.

b Ask them to make a list of 'grounds for discrimination' which could be applied to them. Give them some examples to start them off, e.g. male/female, British/not British, middle-class/working-class, under 25/25 and over. List their suggestions on the board. (This should take about five minutes.)

c Choose one of the pairs of words from the board for students to work on (or ask them to choose one). Get them to sit down in the two groups, e.g. a group of students under 25 and a group aged 25 and over. Give each group a copy of the handout 'Group relations exercise' (see page 99) and ask them to fill it in as a group. (This should take about 15 minutes.)

d When both groups have finished writing, ask them to exchange handouts and talk with each other about what they have written.

e Lead a discussion in which you encourage the students to reflect on the experience of doing the exercise. You could ask them the following questions.

- What were your feelings when you were doing the exercise?
- What did you think of the words that the other group wrote down?
- What do you think this shows about discrimination in the college/ university/outside world?

Handout: group relations exercise

As a group, fill in the following.

Five words which describe our group:

1
2
3
4
5

Five words which describe the other group:

1
2
3
4
5

Five words which we think the other group would use to describe us:

1
2
3
4
5

Chapter 7

Attitudes and values

33 Modelling

34 Teachers' pets

35 Assumptions

36 Self disclosure

37 Rights

Modelling 33

Teachers who are admired and respected by their students are used by them as models. A good way of encouraging equal opportunities is for teachers to set an example to their students in their relationships with one another. Some illustrations follow.

- At the DUET (Development of University English Teaching) workshop on gender at the University of East Anglia in 1988, the teaching staff worked as a co-operative and the assistant administrator was a man, responsible to the woman administrator.

- At the IPR (Interpersonal Process Recall) workshops held annually at Oxford Brookes University until 1993, Norman Kagan used videotapes of black and white women and men in the roles of psychiatrists, doctors, teachers and counsellors.

- Co-counselling courses at the University of the West of England are run jointly by a woman and a man. The woman is responsible for all the training and the man does the paperwork.

Look out for opportunities of sharing power and exchanging traditional roles with your colleagues and encourage your students to learn from your example.

Teachers' pets 34

Though they are seldom fully aware of it, teachers tend to favour not only certain individuals but certain sub-groups from among their students. These preferences are based on attitudes which may be racial, sexual etc. or may be personal to the teacher.

You can find out which students you favour by asking yourself questions about your behaviour. Which students do you pick out for special attention? White men? Blonde women? How do you pick them out? By name? By eye contact? In order to find the answers to these questions you may need to invite a colleague into your classroom to monitor your behaviour. Or you could monitor it yourself if you made a videotape recording of your class. Or, when you get the trust of your students, you could ask them for feedback.

Once you have established where the injustices are, there are several ways of redressing the balance. One is the teach/reteach method which consists of repeatedly recording your classes and analysing the videotapes until you are satisfied that your behaviour has changed. Another is to ask your students to monitor your progress. Or you can institute structures to ensure fairness in at least some aspects of your teaching. For example, if there are particular jobs that students do in your classes, such as arranging the chairs before a seminar (see item 17) or reporting back after a seminar (see item 21) you can draw up a rota so that every student has a regular turn.

In addition, if you institute anonymous marking (see item 27), this will prevent your prejudices affecting the assessment.

Assumptions 35

Students in a group are all too liable to make assumptions about their classmates. A frequent assumption is that they all have similar backgrounds: each student imagines that the others have more in common with her or him than is in fact the case.

For example, white British students – and teachers too – can forget how much of their vocabulary is based in a Christian culture and not realise that references such as 'the Christmas vacation' or 'Christian names' can be alienating, if not hurtful, to others. Similarly the alcohol culture which most students either belong to or at least tolerate can be a barrier for Muslim students who want to get to know their colleagues socially. There may also be invisible differences in the class, such as sexual orientation and certain kinds of disability, e.g. dyslexia, mild hearing impairment.

As a teacher you can give your students a gentle reminder when they start making assumptions. You could say, 'Don't forget that not everyone celebrates Christmas/drinks alcohol' or you could set an example by using the expression 'given names' instead of 'Christian names'. If they make assumptions about sexual orientation by specifying 'wife' or 'husband' or 'girlfriend' or 'boyfriend' you could say, 'I think it would be rash to assume that everyone here is heterosexual. Can we agree to say *partner* or *lover* instead?'

Encourage your students to notice for themselves when such assumptions are being made in the group and invite them to suggest alternative forms of words.

Self disclosure 36

Self disclosure is a crucial factor in the success of any class. Most importantly for equal opportunities, self disclosure by individuals not only helps others to relate to them more easily but also encourages others to be more accepting of the groups to which those individuals belong. For example, if a working-class student shares with her classmates her feelings about being working-class in a middle-class institution, her colleagues will learn not only to empathise with her more as an individual but also to understand more about the situation of other working-class people they meet in the future.

There are various ways in which you can foster self disclosure in your classes. One way is by modelling. You may want to say to your students, for example, 'Since this is the first time we've met, I'd like to tell you that I'm gay. It's bound to affect the way I see things so I think it's best that I tell you from the start. Also I'm not keen on this *Is he or isn't he?* stuff'. Or you may want to share with them some of the difficulties which you faced yourself as a student; a study skills session or an informal conversation may give you the opportunity for this.

Once trust has been established in the group, you can set aside a period of class time for your students – and you – to make personal statements. If these are made in a round, this will ensure that everyone has the opportunity to talk. (For ground rules for rounds see item 18.)

The topic for the round may be collaborative, e.g. 'What I bring to this group' or political, e.g. 'My position as a black/white woman/man' or confronting, e.g. 'What irritates me about the work of this group' or personal, e.g. 'One thing you probably don't know about me'.

Rights 37

People have the right to equal opportunities. But those who have become accustomed to being treated unfairly can find themselves responding with surprise and delight on those occasions when they do receive fair treatment. This has given rise to what commentators on the politics of disability have called 'the gratitude culture'.

If you want to avoid this situation with your students, encourage them to expect equal opportunities as of right and to treat one another fairly as a matter of course. So, for example, men need not congratulate themselves if they accord equal status to a woman. Students should also expect to help a colleague with a disability, not because they are doing her or him a favour but because it is part of their responsibilities as members of the student group to give help when it is needed.

As a teacher you can help your students to be aware of one another's rights in various ways. One way is to give them an explicit reminder. So, to take the first example above, you could say to the man concerned, 'Thank you, John. It's good to see that you acknowledge Jane's right to equal opportunities'. (It would of course be even better if Jane was able to say this to John herself.) Or, in the case of the second example, you could say to the members of the student group, 'Here's a rota of names of students in the group, matched up with week numbers for the academic year. When it's your week, this means that it's your turn to lend your lecture notes to Linda and give her help with anything she misses on account of being deaf'. If any students query this arrangement you could respond by saying 'It's Linda's right to have help from us. We'd do the same for you if you were deaf'.

Chapter 8

Support

Support group 38

Proposing changes and carrying them through, and encouraging others to do the same, can be very stressful and isolating, particularly in such a sensitive area as equal opportunities. It is important that you have the support of other sympathetic people. This can be provided by setting up a self-help support group.

First you will need to identify people who would be interested in forming such a group. You should aim to involve four to six people although support can come from working with just one other person. You may already know people in your institution who share your concerns about discrimination. Alternatively you could advertise an open meeting for interested people.

There are several things which should happen at an initial meeting. First, it is important to stress that the purpose is to set up a *support* group, rather than a group whose main aim is to increase the awareness of discrimination in the institution (though this latter aim may emerge out of the first, see item 52).

Second, examples should be given of some of the many ways in which a staff support group can be used. Initially group members could examine what they do in their own teaching to support equal opportunities (use the item headings in this book for suggestions) and monitor one another's teaching by, for example, sitting in on one another's lectures. The group can then give members support in carrying changes through. Members can celebrate success with the group and use the group as a retreat when things are not going so well.

Third, it is important that the group should itself practise equal opportunity principles, and these should determine how it runs. Overleaf there are a number of suggestions for running the group.

- Avoid a hierarchical structure. Tasks such as chairing meetings, buying and making tea and coffee, writing letters to other interested people should be rotated around the group.

- Do not let one person dominate the group. At the beginning of a meeting each person in turn should have two or three minutes to identify anything she or he would like to share with the group. The group should then decide how to plan the meeting, giving time to those who feel they need it.

- Avoid using discriminatory language. The group members should monitor one another's language.

If you cannot find enough people to form a group, try to pair up with another teacher who is also concerned with countering discrimination in education.

Giving students help 39

Most students will need help of some kind during their education. For some, such as students with disabilities, help may be necessary most of the time. For others, such as a student having difficulties over an essay, support may be needed only until the essay is written. How you help these students may affect how they perceive themselves, and how they are perceived by the other students. It is important that the help you give students maintains, as far as possible, equality within the group.

For a person with a disability you need to consider how that person experiences each teaching situation, what information she or he lacks, and how that information can be provided. The best way of discovering this is to ask the person how you can help. In a classroom situation a person with a visual impairment, for example, is at a disadvantage because she or he will ordinarily miss much of the information which those of us who can see often take for granted: who is in the room; who is being addressed; what is written on the board or projected onto a screen. However there are ways in which the person can be given the information.

- Announce your arrival and say when you are leaving the room.
- Tell her or him who is in the room.
- Ask everyone to say their name when they speak until she or he can recognise everyone's voice.
- Read out, or record onto a cassette, anything that is written.
- Ask people to explain what they are doing if they move around.
- Ask everyone to say the person's name when speaking to her or him.

The situation is different for a student who needs help with an essay. She or he may feel embarrassed about not being able to manage unaided whilst the other students may feel their colleague is less able or that it is unfair that she or he is receiving extra help. One way to make it easier for students to ask for help and to accept others asking for help is to raise the issue at the beginning of the course. Some of the points you may like to make to the students are listed below.

- We all find some tasks easier than others.

- As a result of our different experiences, the tasks which are the easiest for some of us will be the hardest for others.

- Education involves becoming aware of tasks we find difficult and finding ways of making them easier.

- It is often easier to solve a problem by talking about it to another person.

- It is a good thing to ask for help and to share difficulties.

- Help can come from both teachers and students.

This may be an excellent point at which to share some of your own difficulties and ways in which you have been helped (see item 36).

Self help 40

A pitfall for people trying to help oppressed groups is that they can easily slip into patronising behaviour, which is not only insulting but also disempowers the very people they wish to help.

It is in fact difficult not to be patronising if you are a white person teaching racism awareness or a heterosexual arguing for more understanding for lesbians and gays or a man trying to give women equal opportunities in the classroom.

Some groups have come out with statements about how they feel about being patronised. For example, it was the policy of the ITV series *Out on Tuesday* not to explain itself for the benefit of heterosexual viewers. Radical deaf politics rejects theatre for the deaf performed by hearing people. It is also commonplace for groups which are set up for the benefit of women to undertake their own organisation.

If you want to avoid patronising your students, try to encourage and support them instead of organising and protecting them. Help them to see that they can take charge of things themselves. For example, the best people to run a 'return to learning' day for new mature students are members of the students' union who have themselves had the experience of returning to learning. Similarly a blind student is in the best position to act in a supportive capacity for subsequent blind students.

You may need to make a positive move to involve your students and give over your power to them. How you actually do this will depend on your situation and the need being expressed, but the examples which follow indicate some possible forms of words.

- 'There has been a request from some students for a racism awareness workshop. Are there any people here who have had experience of being treated in a racist way who would like to run it? I'd be very interested in helping with ideas of things to do but as a white British person I'd like to share or preferably give over the actual running of the workshop.'

- 'I had no break myself between school and further/higher education and I feel it isn't appropriate for me to run a "return to learning" day for people who have had a break, so I suggest you run the day yourselves. But I can provide you with study skills exercises and book a room for you if that would be helpful.'

Peer pairing 41

For any student, moving to a new educational establishment can be very stressful. But the changes associated with the move will be greater for some students than for others. For example, mature students may not have done any studying for a long time and may be anxious about their ability to cope; students with disabilities may have come from an establishment catering specifically for their needs, and wonder how they will manage in the new environment; students from overseas will have to deal with cultural as well as educational and often linguistic differences.

A way to reduce the stress of the transition is to set up a peer pairing scheme. Under this scheme, established students volunteer to pair up with new students in order to act as guides and friends to them. Most peer pairing programmes are set up to give support to overseas students, though the same service could be offered to any group of students.

At the very least, a peer pairing programme means that the students for whom it is set up know that there is always someone to whom they can turn for help; at best it can foster lasting friendships and academic success. Research carried out as long ago as 1986 on international programmes in Canada[1] suggested that the newcomers benefit from the contact not only personally but also academically. Its very existence, however, can offend if students feel that they have been singled out as members of needy minority groups. One way to overcome this is to pair every new student with an established student.

The simplest version of the scheme involves identifying volunteers, pairing them with the newcomers and leaving them to get on with it. In addition you may like to offer the host students a brief training programme. The following peer pairing programme for overseas students was run at the University of the West of England. You could set up a similar type of programme. If you have never taught interpersonal skills you could perhaps collaborate with the person responsible for overseas students, your student counselling service or colleagues who teach communication and interpersonal skills.

Stage 1 Recruiting the volunteers

In the January before the overseas students arrived, the scheme was outlined to first year lecture groups in departments which take in substantial numbers of overseas students (Law, Engineering). A leaflet describing the scheme was distributed and students were invited to join. The volunteers came from a variety of ethnic backgrounds.

Stage 2 Training the volunteers

In the spring term four training sessions were held, using case studies and experiential learning methods. Five main areas were examined:

- establishing a relationship
- basic counselling skills
- accepting cultural differences
- recognising signs of distress
- using support services

In order to match each volunteer with a newcomer, volunteers were asked to fill in a form (see Figure 2). Students also found the form useful as a basis for conversation when they met their partners.

Stage 3 Bringing the pairs together

At the beginning of the new academic year, a meeting was held for all the new overseas and host students. Here they met their partners and had the opportunity to ask questions and discuss problems. The peer pairing system was described to them, including the provision for changing partners (on either side) or dropping out if they wanted to.

Stage 4 Evaluation

Records were kept of informal feedback and responses to evaluation questionnaires. The academic progress made by the overseas students was also followed.

This item was written with the help of Eira Makepeace, Centre for Student Affairs, University of the West of England.

[1] M. J. Westwood et al., 'New dimensions in orientation of international students' in J. Mestenhauser (ed), *Orientation Programmes for International Students*, Intercultural Press, New York, 1986.

Figure 2: Form used in peer pairing scheme

UK Pairs Details

Please complete this form to help us find you an appropriate partner.

Name ______________________ Age ________ Gender ________

Course ____

Address (term time) ______________________________________

____

Home address ____

____

Phone number ____

Do you have a car? ____

What are your hobbies and interests? _____________________________

____

____

What sports do you enjoy? ____________________________________

____

What languages do you speak? _________________________________

What work experience have you had? ____________________________

____

What countries have you visited? ________________________________

____

Do you have any preferences for matching (e.g. nationality, gender)?

____

What attracts you to this scheme? ______________________________

____

Providing support facilities 42

Certain people may be prevented from applying to your institution, not because they do not have the appropriate entry qualifications, but because they require particular support facilities which are not available. For example, there may be no crèche for a parent with a preschool child, no ramps for someone who needs to use a wheelchair, or no special aids for a person with a visually impairment. Such people are likely to be in the minority and, in their absence, unable to fight for the necessary provision. The demand for the provision of such facilities is however the responsibility of everyone.

Make a list of the support facilities you can identify in your establishment. A useful (if frustrating) way to test the facilities is to put yourself in the position of someone with a special need. For example, you could borrow a pram or wheelchair and try to get around between and within buildings. For this really to work you need to be prepared to do it for an entire day. You may be surprised at what you discover! It may be less easy to test other support facilities, but you can discuss them with relevant people: the librarian, the computer unit, people with special needs etc. Find out whether other courses have accepted people with special needs and talk to the relevant staff about provision.

An alternative to doing this yourself is to run it as a student exercise, especially if the students are taking a relevant course, for example social studies, nursing, social work, life skills. The students should work in groups of two or three, each group putting themselves in the place of people with a particular need. Their task is to identify which facilities are provided and which are not. Give the students a week to collect their information, after which they should report back their findings at a meeting of the whole group. Compile two lists, one of the existing facilities, one of facilities which are not available. Use the following suggestions as a checklist.

- ramps for access by wheelchairs and pushchairs to all buildings, teaching rooms, social and eating areas etc.
- doors which can be opened with ease by people in a wheelchair, or using crutches etc.
- doors and aisles which are wide enough to accommodate a wheelchair
- lifts to all floors in all buildings
- toilets for wheelchair users
- crèche for children of students and staff
- feeding and changing facilities for parents with young children
- half-term and school holiday provision for school children
- large scale magnifiers in the library
- signers for people using sign language
- teaching rooms with induction loops for people with hearing aids
- fiche and computer screens with adjustments to cope with visual problems
- tables with height/angle adjustments for people using wheelchairs
- readers for people with visual impairments
- computer terminal access for people who are unable to use a pen
- braille signs on doors

This is, of course, only the beginning. Two things need to follow. First, you may have discovered support services of which you were unaware and your institution needs to be encouraged to advertise the availability of these facilities. The most important people to inform are prospective students and staff involved in admissions. Check the prospectus. If the facilities are not mentioned there, suggest that they should be, perhaps in a separate section (see item 1). Talk to the person in overall charge of admissions. Suggest that a handout on people with special needs is written and sent to all admissions tutors.

Second, you need to pass on information about facilities which are not provided. Be prepared for resistance when you try to do this, and the argument that priority has to be given to facilities for majority groups. Try to get the support of sympathetic people (see item 38). You may find however that it is difficult to get any improvement in provision until the institution is faced with a student who has particular needs which are not being met.

Getting outside help 43

You and your colleagues don't need to feel you must solve all your students' problems internally. There are national and local organisations which have the experience and expertise – and sometimes funds – to give you and your students the help you need.

These include, for example, the Equal Opportunities Commission (EOC), the Council for Racial Equality (CRE), the Royal National Institute for the Blind (RNIB), the Royal Association for Disability and Rehabilitation (RADAR) etc. You can find their addresses and telephone numbers in the telephone book, or from the Citizens' Advice Bureau, local library, Health Education Unit etc. There is also a list of useful addresses at the end of this book.

To illustrate the kind of support these groups can offer: the RNIB can, given sufficient notice, provide audio-tapes of prescribed reading for blind students and your local branch of the Royal Society for the Blind can give advice and help with the purchase of aids, such as the talking calculator. Or, to give another example, the EOC and CRE will support a student who is treated in a discriminatory way at an interview for a job or course.

Representatives of these groups may also be willing – or even keen – to come as guest speakers to your department to describe their work or discuss particular issues with students and staff. You could also consider asking outside experts to run workshops for your students in, for example, racism awareness, assertiveness or careers for mature graduates.

In addition, help is available from the Students' Union. You will find that not only is the Welfare Officer very helpful in a general way but also that the Union caters for specific groups through such organisations as the Mature Students' Union, to which the National Union of Students is affiliated.

You can also get help from other institutions. For example, Manchester Metropolitan University produces a *Mature Students' Handbook* which offers information and advice to prospective mature students and includes case studies of individuals who have been successful. Copies of the handbook are available from The Registry, Manchester Metropolitan University, All Saints, Manchester, M15 6BH, telephone 0161 247 2000.

Providing interview experience 44

All of your students are going to leave your institution sooner or later and, because of their different backgrounds and types of experience, some of them will be better able than others to cope with any interviews they may have. Some students may have never had an interview; others may have had experience of interviews but not recently; others again may feel anxious about how they will deal with particular questions.

One way you can help your students move on successfully is to give them the opportunity beforehand to develop their interview skills and to explore those aspects of the interview they may never have experienced or feel they will find difficult. Before you embark on this you will need to find out what is likely to be required of them in interviews for particular sorts of jobs or careers. Your careers officer may be able to help you with this. Some of the skills which may be assessed at an interview include writing reports, leading a discussion, collaborating with other people and summarising an argument as well as answering interview questions clearly and concisely.

You can help your students by providing them with practical experience of these situations. For example, you could set up mock interviews with yourself and one or two of your colleagues as the interviewers. You could ask the students some discriminatory questions (e.g. about child care arrangements for mature students) to give them practice in dealing with discrimination in interviews. If the students agree, it can be very useful to video-tape the 'interviews' and to let each student view her or his tape.

You could also provide small groups of students with practice in leading discussions and summarising arguments, again using video playback to give them feedback.

Chapter 9

Responding to discrimination

'How do you feel about that?' 45

One way of responding to discrimination is to say how it makes you feel. You may want to say, for example, 'When you look at me like that, I feel angry' or 'When you describe us like that, I feel inferior to you' or 'Being addressed like that makes me feel uncomfortable; I'd prefer it if you didn't use that sort of language'. The advantage of this method of responding is that, though people may claim that you are foolish to have these feelings, they cannot deny that you have them. Once they discover how you feel, this may give them some insight into how their behaviour affects others.

If a student in the classroom makes a discriminatory remark about a colleague in the class, you can ask the second student 'How do feel about that?' If she or he replies honestly, there is a much better chance that the first student – and others in the class – will learn something than if you rush in with a challenge yourself: students can learn more easily from one another and a statement of feelings has an impact all of its own.

'I notice . . .' 46

This use of the expression'I notice . . .' is borrowed from Gestalt therapy where it is used by the therapist to give a client feedback which is descriptive rather than interpretative.

You may want to give your students feedback about some aspect of their classroom behaviour but you may prefer to leave them the responsibility of deciding how they interpret it and how they want to deal with it. In that case it is usually sufficient to say, for example, 'I notice that all the overseas students are sitting together' or 'I notice that no women have spoken yet in this seminar'.

If you are worried that your students may find such comments so threatening as to be counterproductive, you could warn them at the beginning of the course or session that it is your intention to offer descriptive feedback of this kind. You could also involve them in the process by inviting them to comment on what they see and hear, using the same formula, 'I notice . . .'

'That's a racist remark.' 47

One of the most straightforward ways of responding to discriminatory behaviour is to show, by giving it a name, that you recognise it for what it is. You can say, quite simply, 'That's a racist remark' or 'That's a sexist joke'. This is a clearer and more direct way of responding than the cautious 'Sounds a bit racist to me' or the sarcastic 'Some people round here have never heard of equal opportunities' or the angry 'Don't be so bloody classist!'

If you decide that you want to name discrimination when you encounter it, be prepared to explain yourself since the other person may not at first recognise it as such. If the explanation is equally clear and direct, this should discourage both you and the other person from being driven into aggressive or defensive positions. The kind of explanation you might want to give is 'When you said that about mature students, you were speaking about them in a general way as if they weren't individuals' or 'The point of your anecdote is that the student turned out to be gay; you are implying that homosexuality is abnormal'.

You will not always convince the person there and then but she or he may go away and think about what you have said. And if you persevere in naming discriminatory behaviour on the part of your colleagues and students, they will come to anticipate your comments and be more likely to choose to express themselves differently.

'What do you mean?' 48

A lot of discriminatory behaviour is presented in the form of jokes, innuendoes, hints or suggestive gestures. Sometimes these are malicious but more often they arise from thoughtlessness or habit. Simply asking students or colleagues to explain themselves can be enough in itself to discourage them from behaving in this way again on another occasion.

The kind of question you might want to ask is, for example, 'Can you explain that to me?' or 'Why are you winking at me?' or, simply, 'What do you mean?' Don't be content with the reply 'It's only a joke': ask 'Can you explain to me what the joke is?' or 'Why is that funny?'

These questions, simple as they are, are very confronting. If the joke is stripped away, people are faced with the real implications of what they are saying or of how they are behaving. You need to be prepared for strong reactions if you use this method of responding.

'Would you say that to a man?' 49

Many people are genuinely unaware of ways in which their behaviour is discriminatory; they may generalise about black people or joke about disability or leer at women, without thinking about what they are doing. One way of helping your colleagues and students to recognise when their behaviour is discriminatory is to ask them if they would behave in the same way towards someone from a different group. This can show people the way they differentiate between groups and help them to see what their hidden assumptions are. For example, depending on what the other person said, you might respond:

- 'Would you say that to a man?'
- 'Would you speak to me like that if we were the same age?'
- 'What difference does his colour make?'
- 'Would it be the same if I said that to you?'
- 'Would you speak to the head of department the way you just spoke to the secretary?'

'That's just an excuse.' 50

Sometimes, when challenged, people attempt to back up their discriminatory behaviour with elaborate justifications and rationalisations. They may say, for example, 'It's very cumbersome to say "he or she" every time' or 'I've got nothing against homosexuals but I don't see why they think they can appropriate the word "gay" '.

If you respond to the presenting argument and, in the case of the above examples, engage in a theoretical discussion about the uses of language, there is a danger that you will lose sight of the underlying discriminatory intention of the original comments. It will be more effective if you go straight to the point and say 'That's just an excuse' or 'That sounds to me like an excuse'.

Similarly, if colleagues in your department argue that you can't take on students with disabilities because you don't have the facilities, you could say 'That sounds like an excuse to me. Facilities aren't difficult to arrange. Perhaps it would be a good idea if we looked at people's real reasons for not wanting students with disabilities'.

'What do the rest of you think?' 51

You don't have to undertake all your equal opportunities struggles alone. There are generally other people around who see things your way. All they need is a little encouragement before they will speak up in your support.

If you are faced with discriminatory behaviour in a class or meeting, rather than dealing with it single-handed, try asking the other people present, 'What do the rest of you think?' This will open up the debate and encourage others to speak out against discrimination.

In certain situations you can also ask this question in writing. For example, people in educational institutions often make public, if anonymous, declarations of their prejudices by writing graffiti on notices or displays. This seems to happen particularly in relation to racism. The most common response on the part of the person who mounted the display is to dismantle it and destroy the evidence in an attempt to protect those who are the target of the attack. An alternative strategy, however, is to put up a second display consisting of the original material, mounted on a poster with the caption: 'The above was defaced while on display in this department. What is your reaction? Staff and students are invited to write their comments below'. An advantage of this type of display is that it encourages passers-by to participate in the debate. When this method was used in the Faculty of Education at the University of the West of England, it elicited a reassuring number of critical comments and constructive suggestions (for example, requests for more racism awareness workshops).

Secondly, there are still plenty of pin-ups and sexist calendars etc. to be seen in public areas in educational institutions, as well as the more recent appearance of computer images of nude women. Again, rather than tearing them down or arguing with the men who displayed them you could put up a notice inviting people to state in writing how they feel about them.

Chapter 10

Going public

52 Spreading the word

53 Setting up a working party

Spreading the word 52

One of the aims of any teacher who believes in equal opportunities must be to make others aware of the importance of this issue. If your aim is to influence other people's attitudes and values, you will want to spread the word as widely as possible and publicise your discoveries and arguments.

You can do this either by producing material yourself or by disseminating the work of other people, or by setting up an equal opportunities working party of some kind (see item 53).

You can write articles about discrimination in your institution and publish them in a house magazine or newsletter. For example, Elizabeth Miles at Bristol Polytechnic in the 1980's wrote an article entitled 'Academic mothers at Bristol Polytechnic' for *Poly News* (volume 5) and the Senate Sex Equality Committee produced 'Are you man enough . . .?' for *University of Warwick Newsletter* (number 104). Or you can ask your students to write about their experiences, e.g. a student with a disability could write a set of guidelines for teachers. Or you can produce more general material, such as an article for a journal or a letter to a newspaper, and try to get it published nationally. (For example, J. Dain, 'Getting women into computing', *University Computing*, 10, 154-157, 1988.)

If you come across a good article about equal opportunities in a journal or newspaper, show it to your colleagues and ask them for their views, or alternatively apply to the publisher for permission to reproduce it for your institution.

Setting up a working party 53

If you want to make progress with equal opportunities within your department or across the institution as a whole, you should enlist the support of sympathetic staff and students and set up a working party with the particular brief to look at equal opportunities; it could be attached to a union or to a departmental or institutional committee and would serve a more formal but complementary function to that of a support group (see item 38).

The members of the working party could concern themselves with any of a variety of methods of promoting equal opportunities.

- You could organise workshops in such areas as assertiveness training or racism awareness. These workshops could be run either by internal members with experience of such work or by facilitators from outside the institution.

- You could investigate the politics of the institution, looking at, for example, who gets promoted, how decisions are made in meetings, or which course proposals are accepted and why.

- You could find out what written statements of equal opportunities policy there are in your department or institution and publicise them or, in their absence, write them. You can base them on existing statements which groups in other institutions have drawn up. Statements of policy are important, particularly since research indicates that colleges with a written policy on disability have more students with special educational needs than those without such a policy. Though it is not clear which came first, the students or the policy, a written policy, even if it is weakly supported by resources, provides a fulcrum for future change[1].

- You could persuade your institution to make a commitment to the cause of equal opportunities by including it as a criterion for staff appraisal and promotion.

- You could publicise or devise grievance procedures.

[1] Paul Abberley, 'More than a policy: Disabled students and the Polytechnic', *Poly News*, Bristol Polytechnic, Summer 1989.

Addresses[1]

The British Dyslexia Institute
98 London Road
Reading
RG1 5AU
Tel: 01734 668271

Commission for Racial Equality
Elliot House,
10-12 Allington Street
London
SW1E 5EH
Tel: 0171 828 7022

The Engineering Council
(Women into Science & Engineering)
10 Maltravers Street
London WC2R 3ER
Tel: 0171 240 7891

Equal Opportunities Commission
Overseas House,
Quay Street
Manchester
M3 3HN
Tel: 0161 833 9244

1 Correct at the time of publication.

Gay Switchboard
Tel: 0171 837 7324

Gingerbread Association for One Parent Families
49 Wellington Street
London
WC2E 7BN
Tel: 0171 240 0953

Mobility Trust
4 Hughes Mews,
143A Chatham Road
London
SW11 6HJ
Tel: 0171 924 3597

National Bureau for Students With Disabilities (SKILL)
336 Brixton Road
London
SW9 7AA
Tel: 0171 274 0565

Physically Handicapped and Able Bodied (PHAB)
12-14 London Road
Croydon
CRO 2TA
Tel: 0181 667 9443

Royal Association for Disability and Rehabilitation (RADAR)
25 Mortimer Street
London
W1N 8AB
Tel: 0171 250 3222

Royal National Institute for the Blind (RNIB)
Education Department
224 Great Portland Street
London
W1N 6AA
Tel: 0171 388 1266

Royal National Institute for the Deaf (RNID)
105 Gower Street
London
WC1E 6AH
Tel: 0171 387 8033